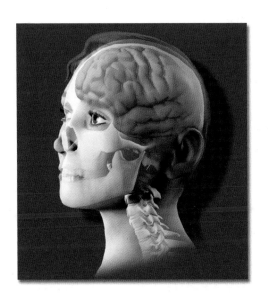

The Brain

Ben Williams

Table of Contents

The World's Fastest Computer

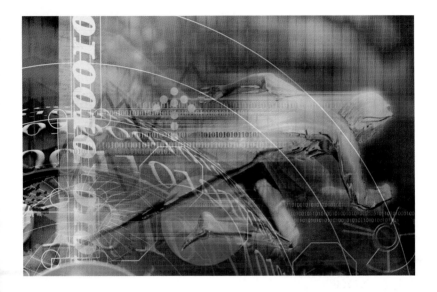

There is an amazing computer. It is faster than any other computer in the world. It can understand speech and writing. It can come up with new ideas. It can make plans. It can control a whole, complicated system and do many things at once without shutting down.

In fact, the more it is used, the better it seems to get.

What is this amazing computer? It is your brain, of course!

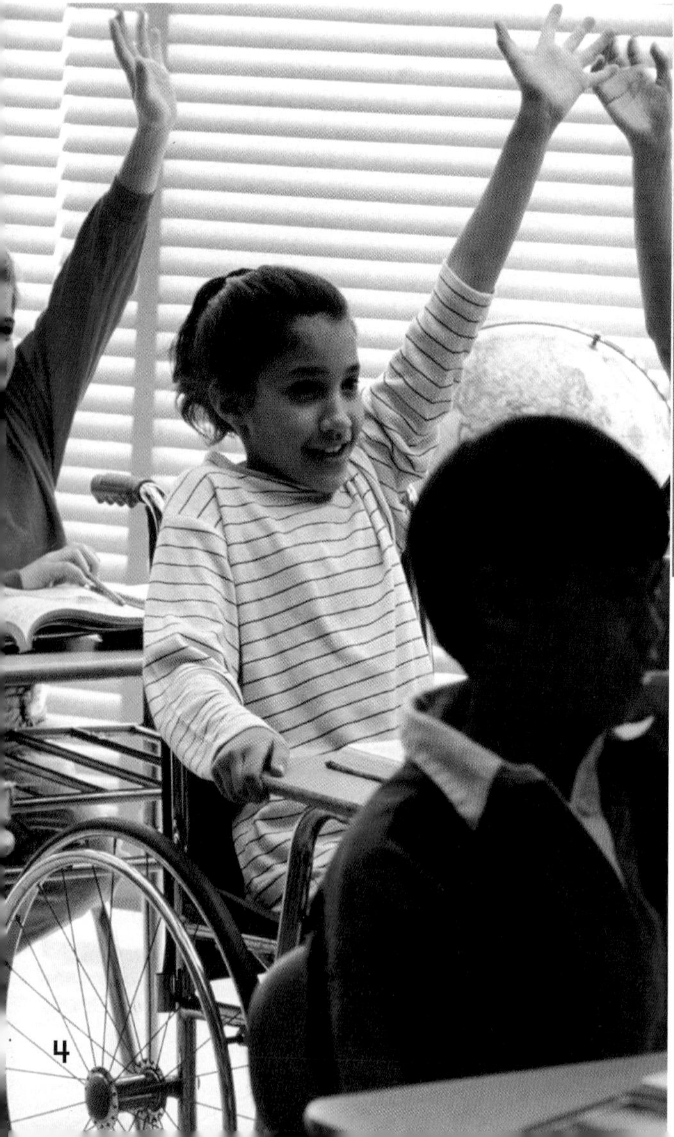

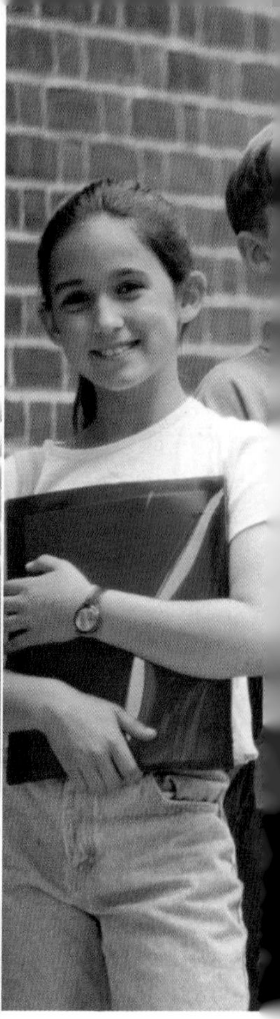

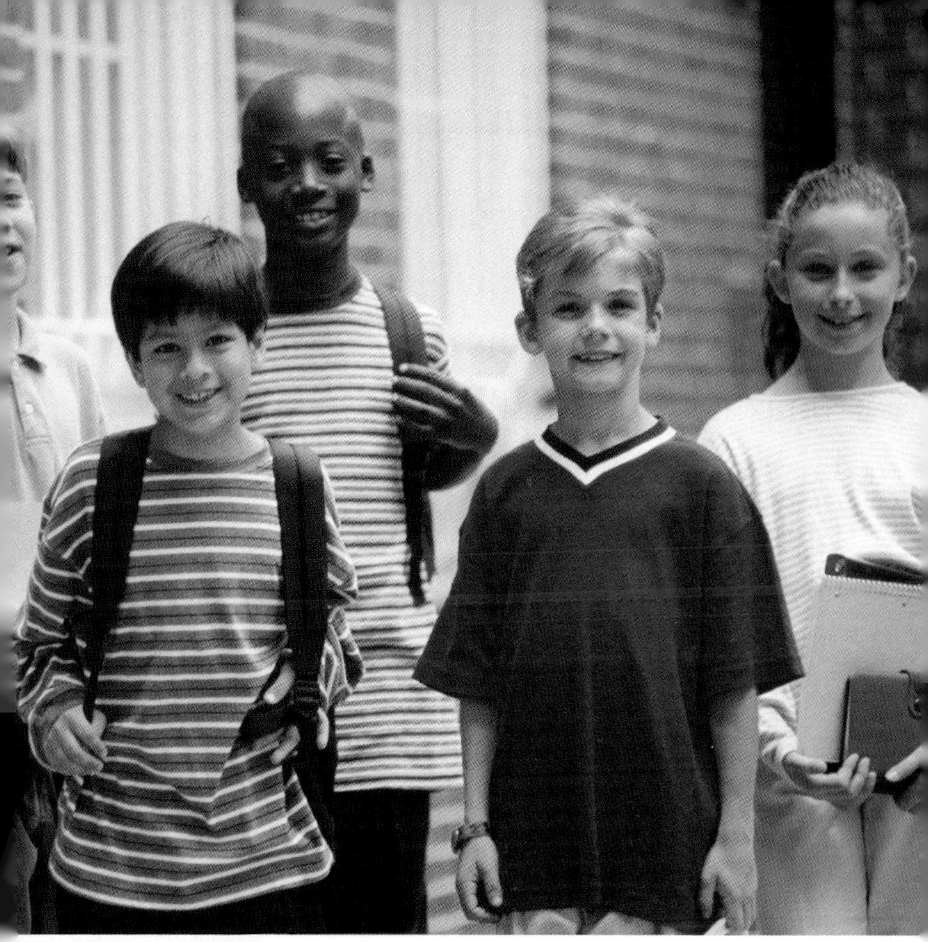

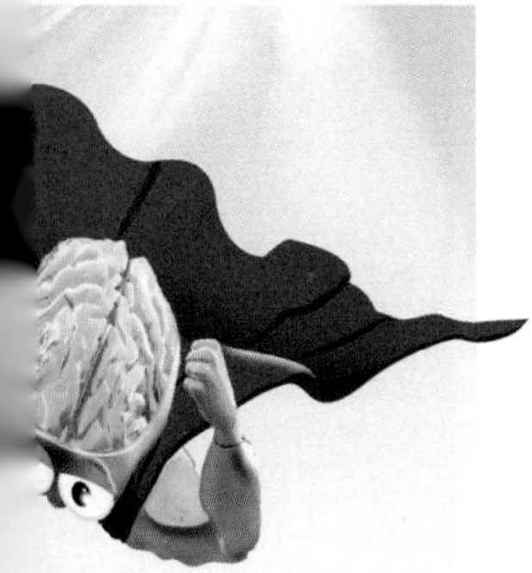

Superbrain!

How fast is your brain? Some people say that it can handle 10 quadrillion instructions each second. That's 10,000,000,000,000,000!

What Is a Brain?

Most animals have a brain. But your brain—the human brain—is the most amazing brain of all. It is larger and more complicated than other brains.

The human brain sits inside the skull at the top and back of the head. It is about the size of a small cauliflower, and it is shaped a little like one, too.

The brain is very important. That is why it is protected inside the hard skull bones.

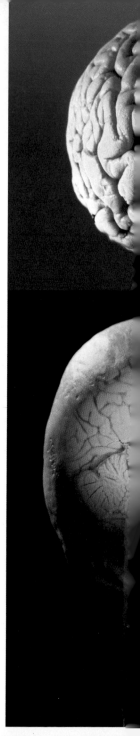

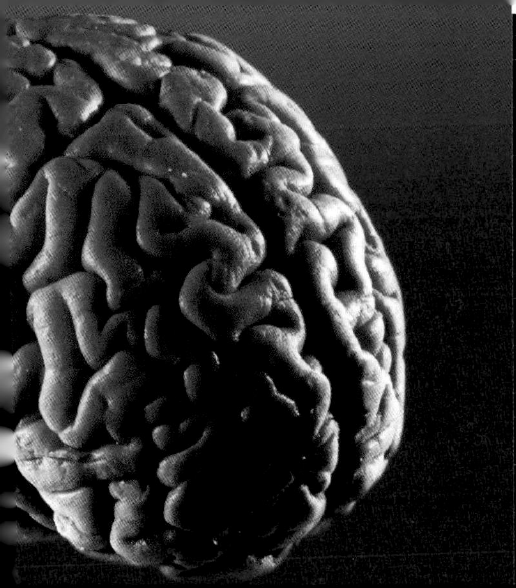

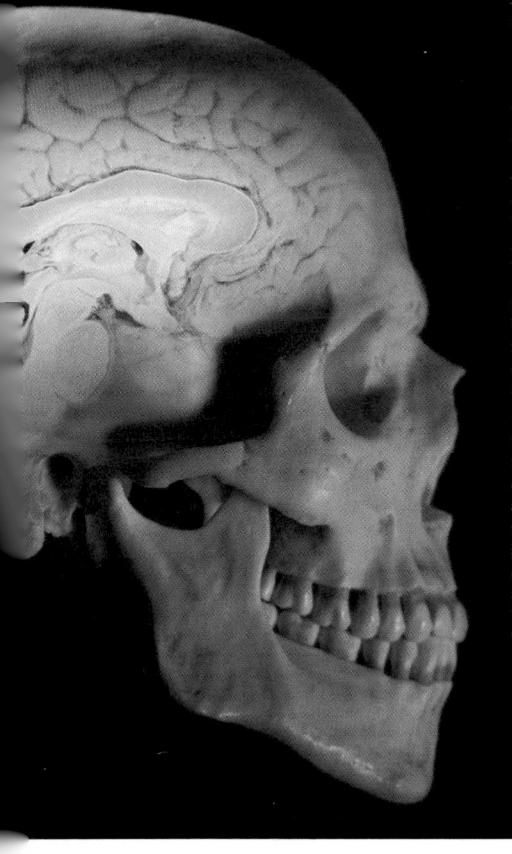

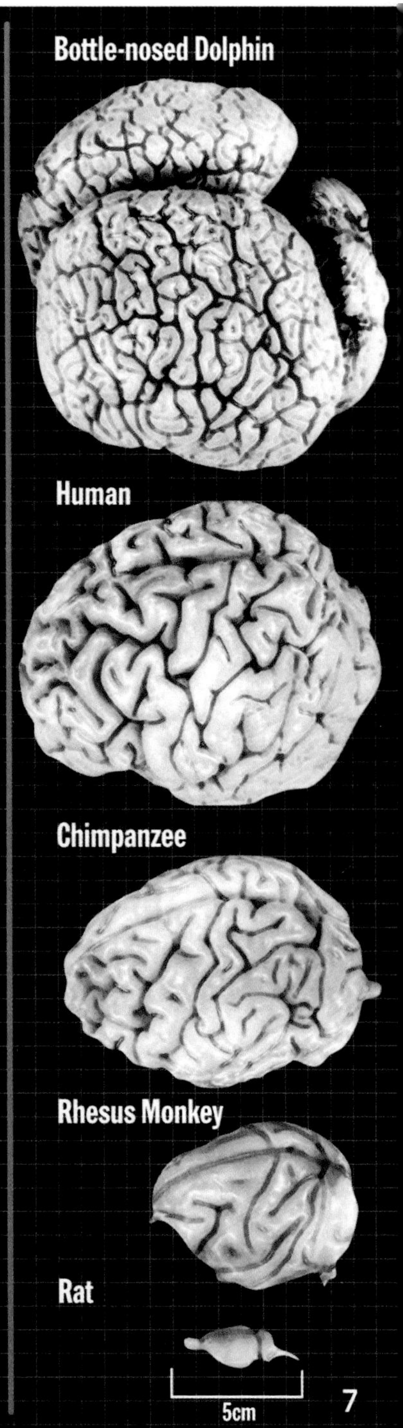
Bottle-nosed Dolphin
Human
Chimpanzee
Rhesus Monkey
Rat
5cm

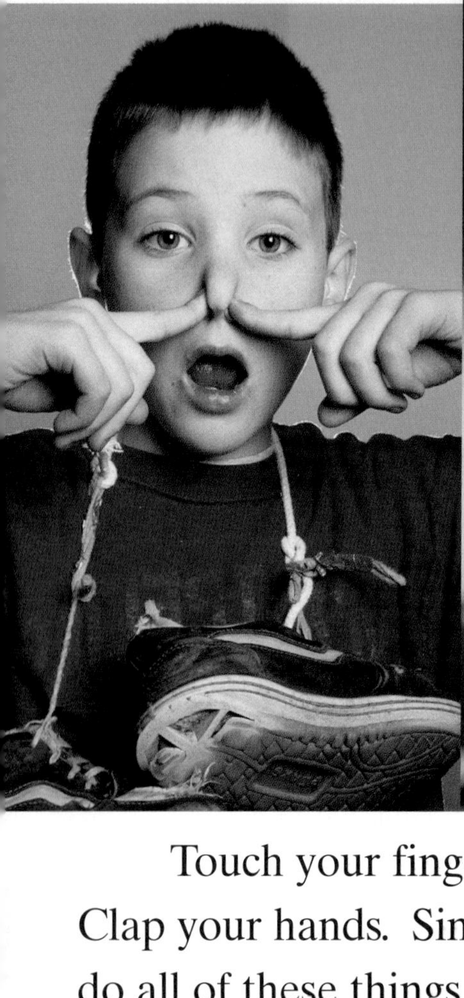

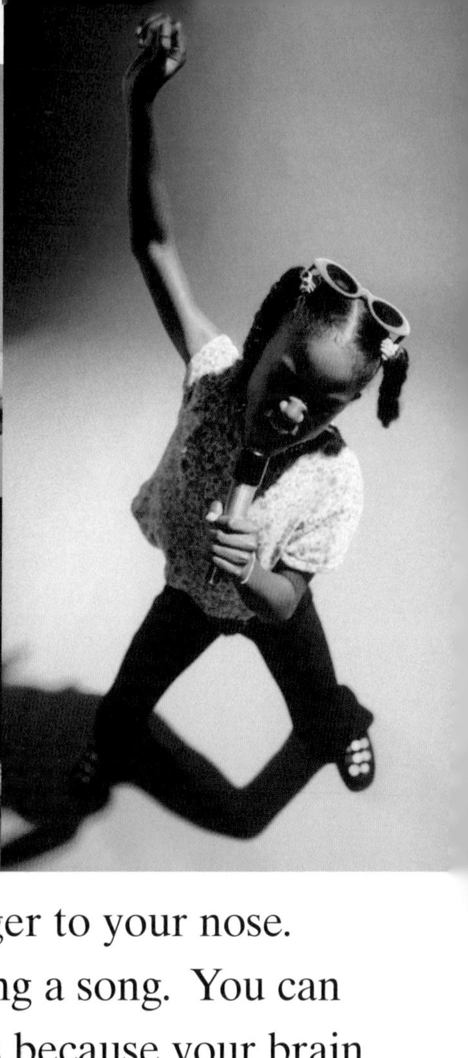

Touch your finger to your nose. Clap your hands. Sing a song. You can do all of these things because your brain tells your body what to do.

Your brain is always on the job. It is like a boss and all the parts of your body are the workers. All you have to do is

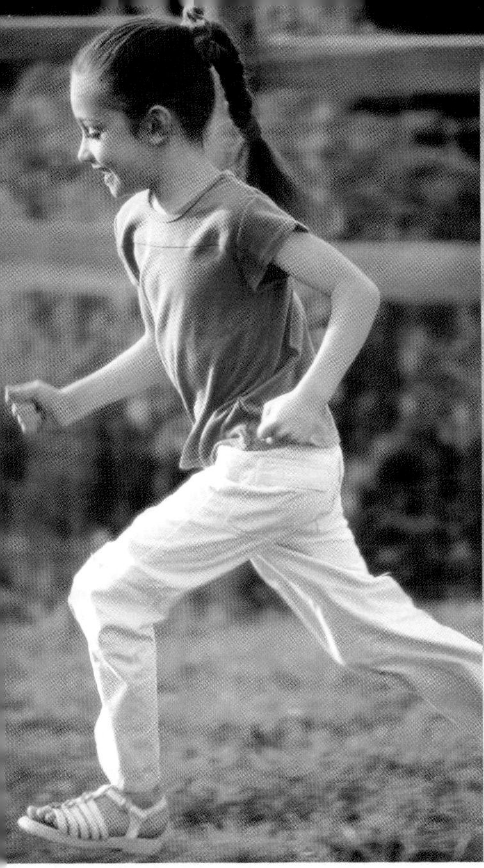
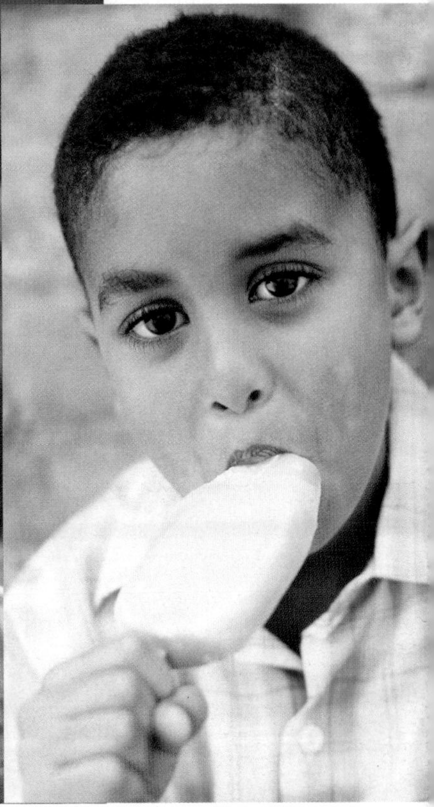

think a thought, and your brain makes the workers get right to work.

For example, if you want to run, your brain thinks, "Run," and your legs and feet do their jobs. If you want to eat, your brain sends a message to all the right parts. Just like that, you are eating.

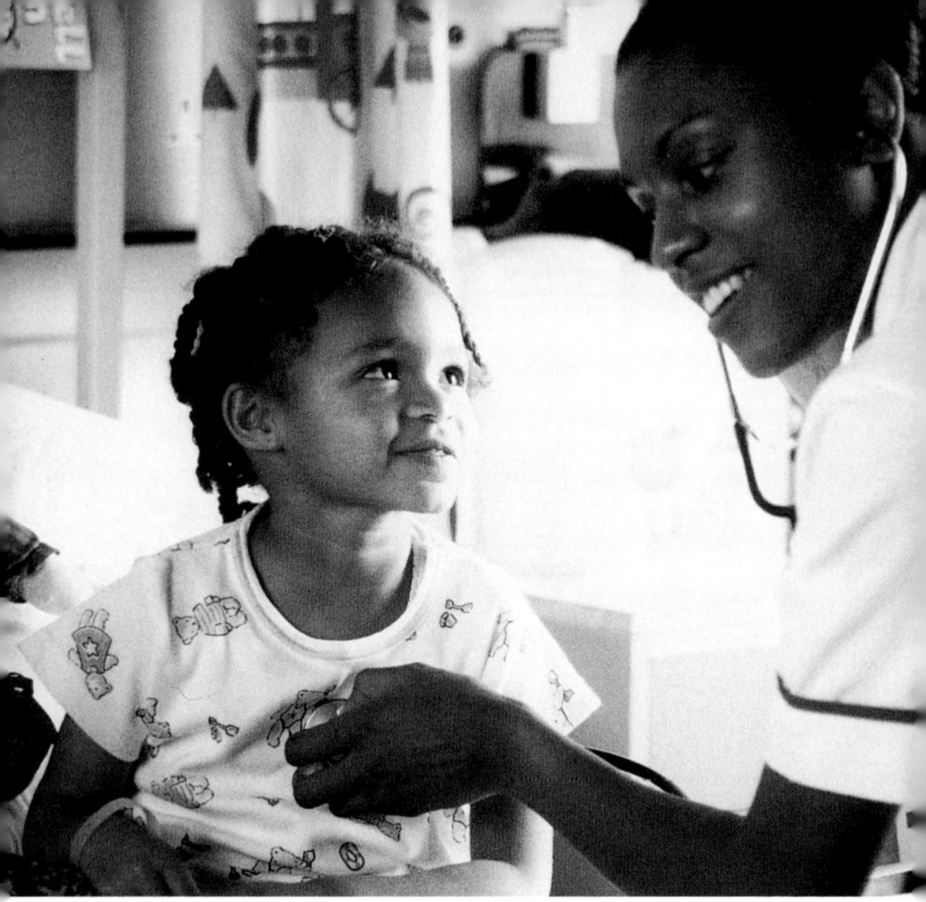

Your brain is so amazing that it can make your body do some things without you needing to think about them. You breathe without thinking. Your heart beats without thinking. Your body temperature stays just right. These are just some of the things your brain handles on its own.

Who's in Charge?

You can think about breathing and then do it, but you do not have to. Your brain will keep you breathing whether you think about it or not.

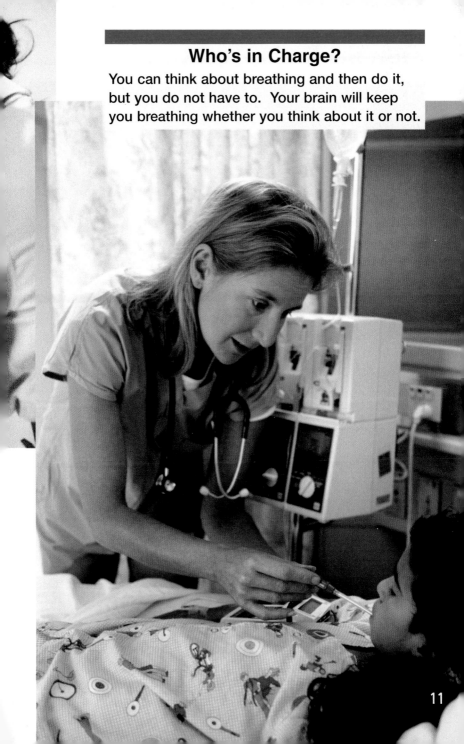

How the Brain Works

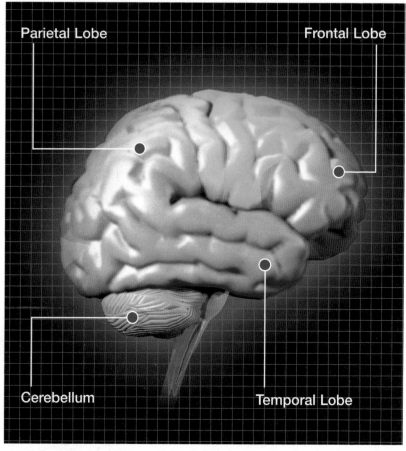

Parietal Lobe

Frontal Lobe

Cerebellum

Temporal Lobe

The brain is part of the nervous system. It works with the spinal cord and the nerves. They work together to control, balance, and keep the body, mind, and emotions in order.

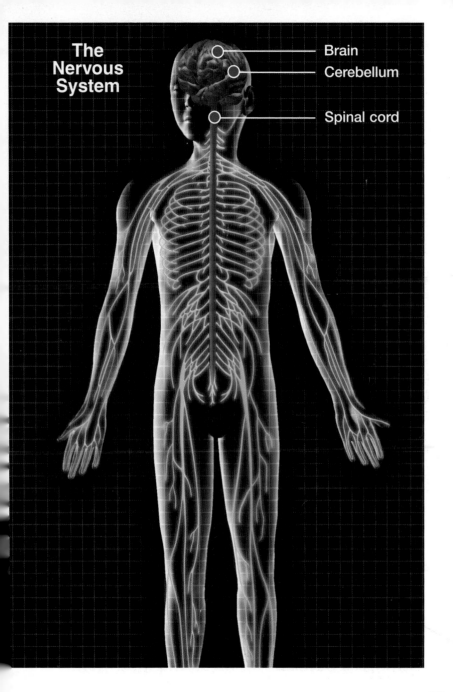

The
Nervous
System

Brain

Cerebellum

Spinal cord

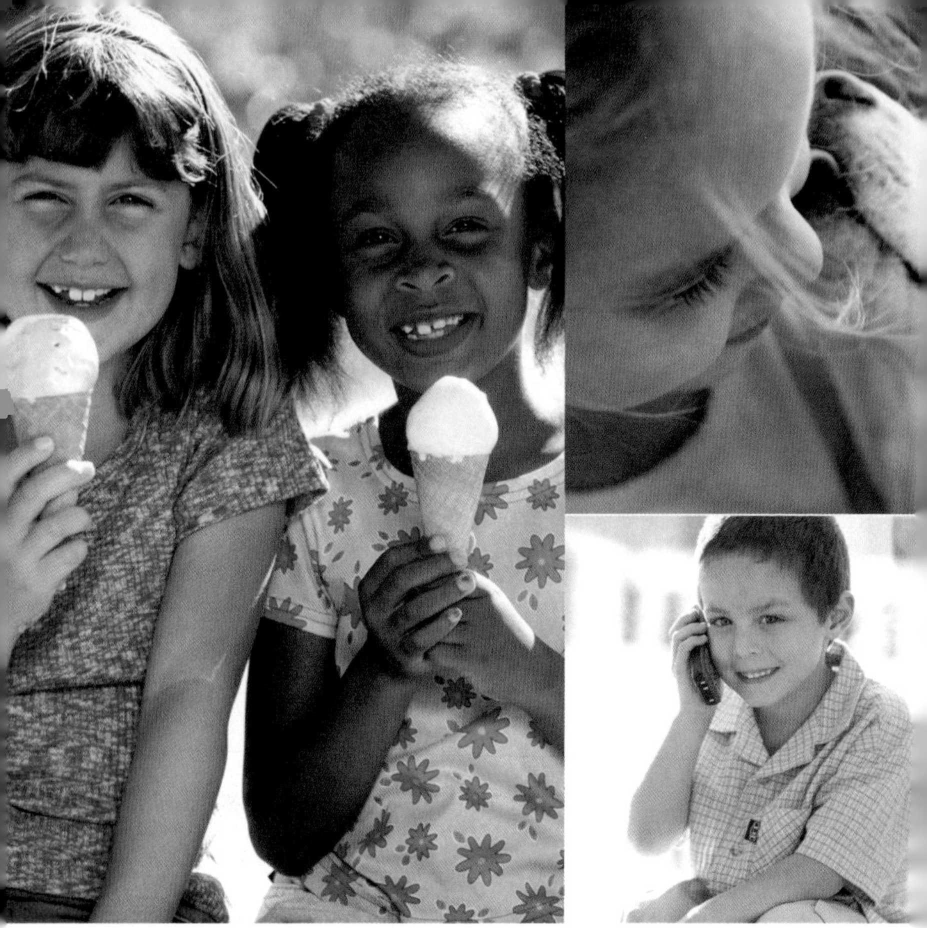

The brain takes information from outside the body. Then it sends the information through the body, using the nervous system.

To get information, the brain uses the five **senses**: sight, hearing, touch, smell, and taste.

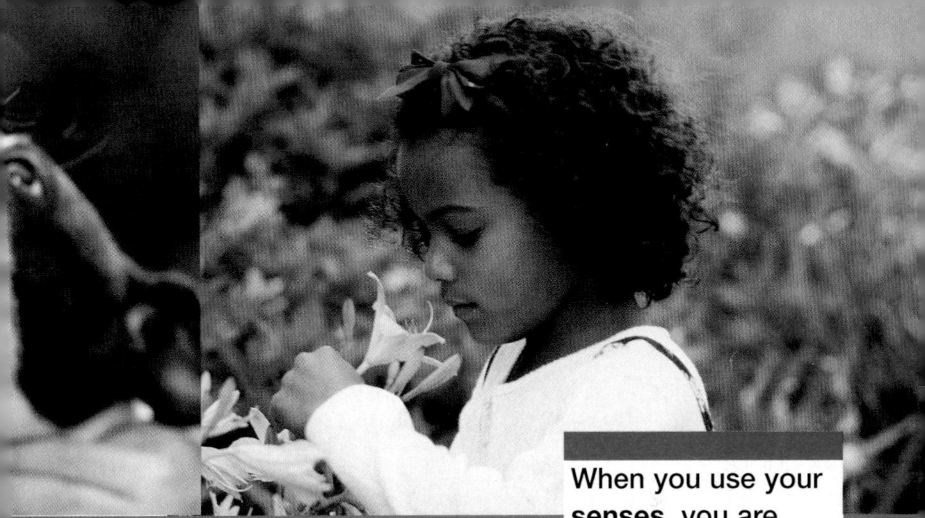

When you use your **senses**, you are using your brain.

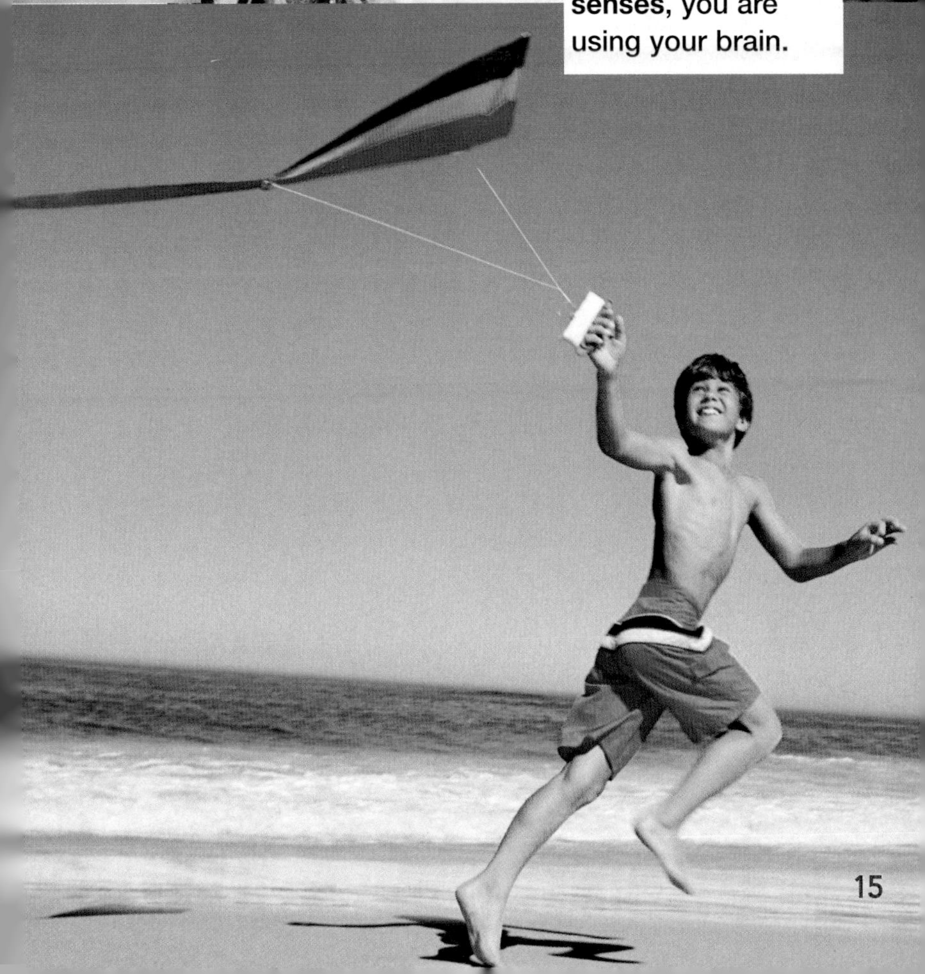

To send information, the brain uses **neurons**. Neurons are nerve cells. They can be found throughout the body. They send messages to each other.

Each neuron is made of three main parts: **cell body**, **axon**, and **nerve ending**.

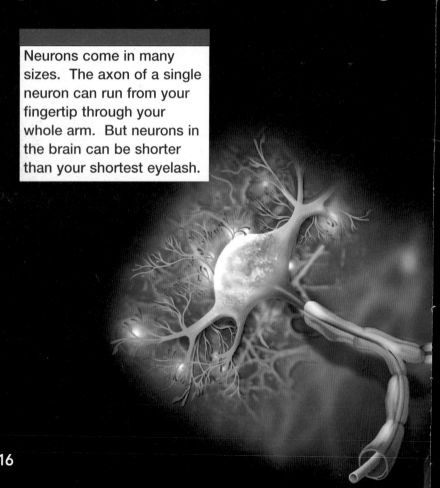

Neurons come in many sizes. The axon of a single neuron can run from your fingertip through your whole arm. But neurons in the brain can be shorter than your shortest eyelash.

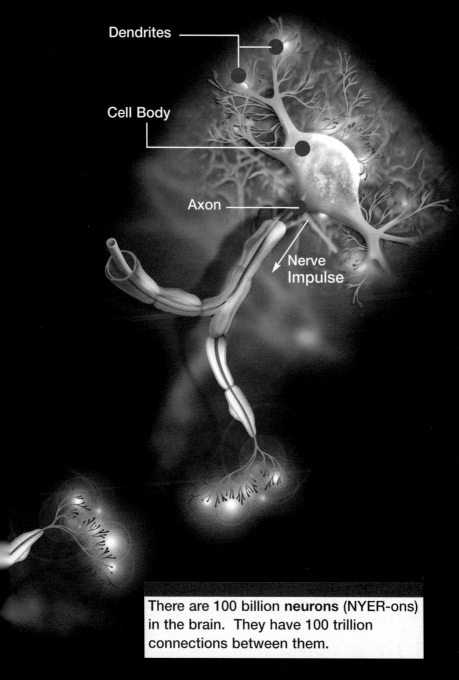

Dendrites

Cell Body

Axon

Nerve
Impulse

There are 100 billion **neurons** (NYER-ons)
in the brain. They have 100 trillion
connections between them.

Parts of the Brain

The brain is made of the **brainstem**, the **cerebellum** (ser-e-Bel-em), and the **forebrain**.

The brainstem is in charge of the things we do without thinking, like breathing. It is also in charge of moving our arms and legs, digesting food, and getting rid of waste.

The cerebellum makes the parts of our body work together so that we stay balanced.

The forebrain controls our body temperature and our emotions. It puts together the information it gets from the senses. It holds our memories for us, and it lets us think.

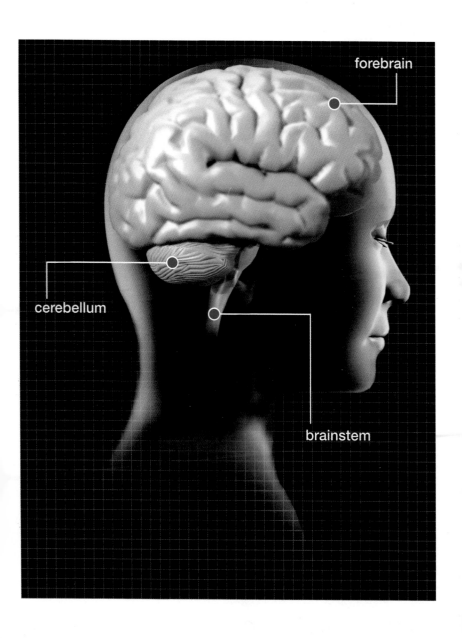

forebrain

cerebellum

brainstem

Use Your Noodle

Has anyone ever told you to use your noodle? Have they said, "Put on your thinking cap"? These are just two of the funny names people use for the brain. They tell us to keep thinking.

It is important to use our brains when we want to do something. The

brain will tell us how to do it. It will tell us if it is right or wrong, and it will tell us if it is safe.

If you are not sure about something, just use your noodle! It will help you figure it out.

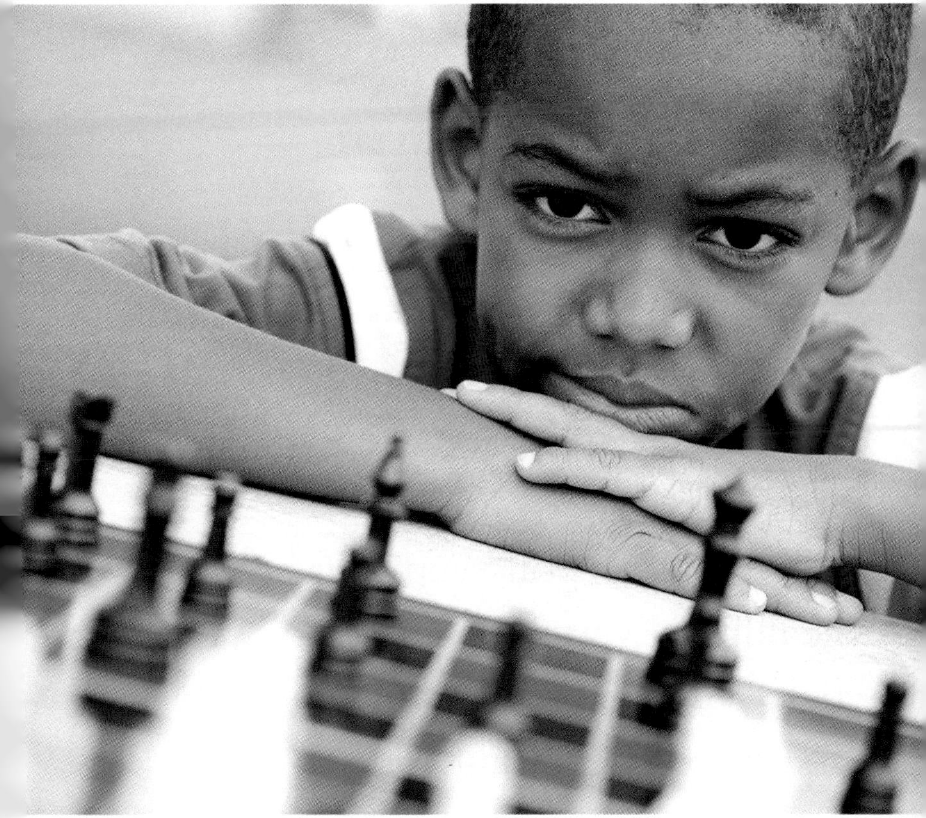

A Healthy Brain

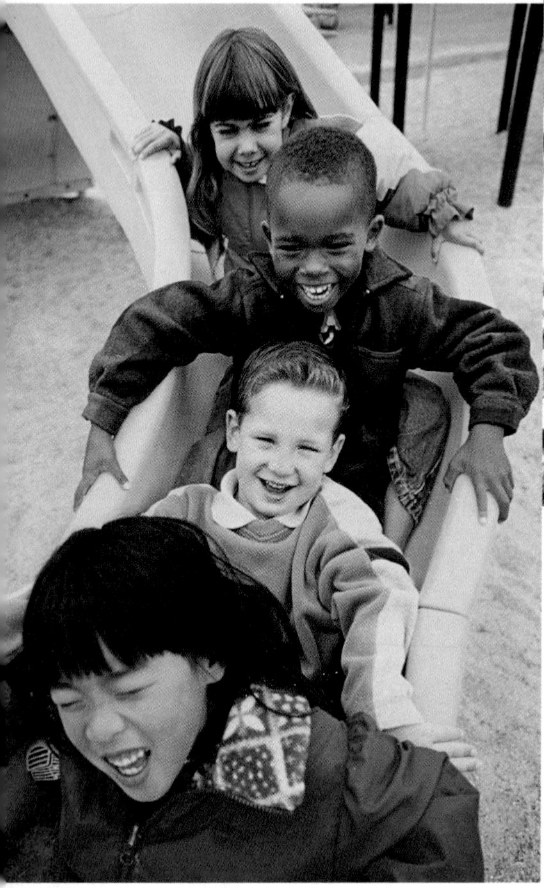

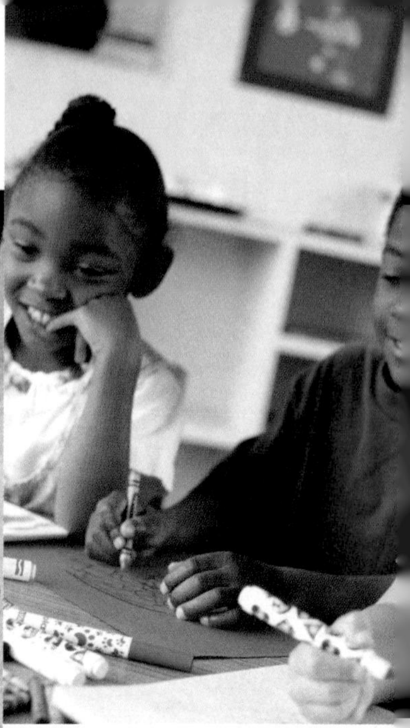

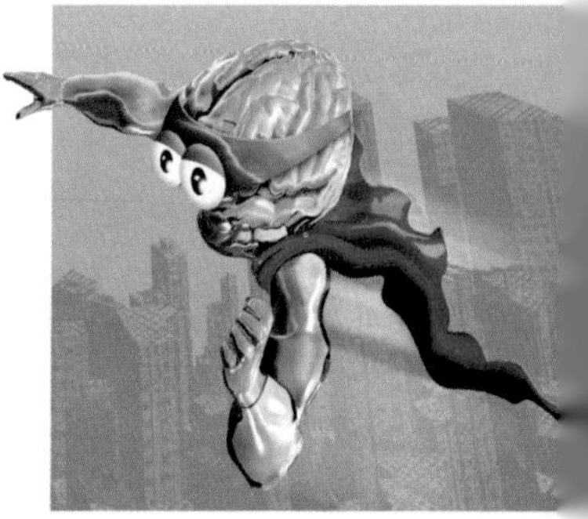

How can you keep your brain healthy? Everything in the body works best with good food and lots of water. Exercise is important, too.

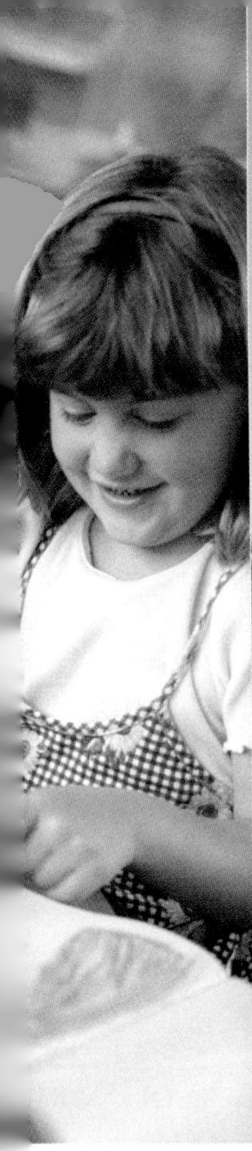
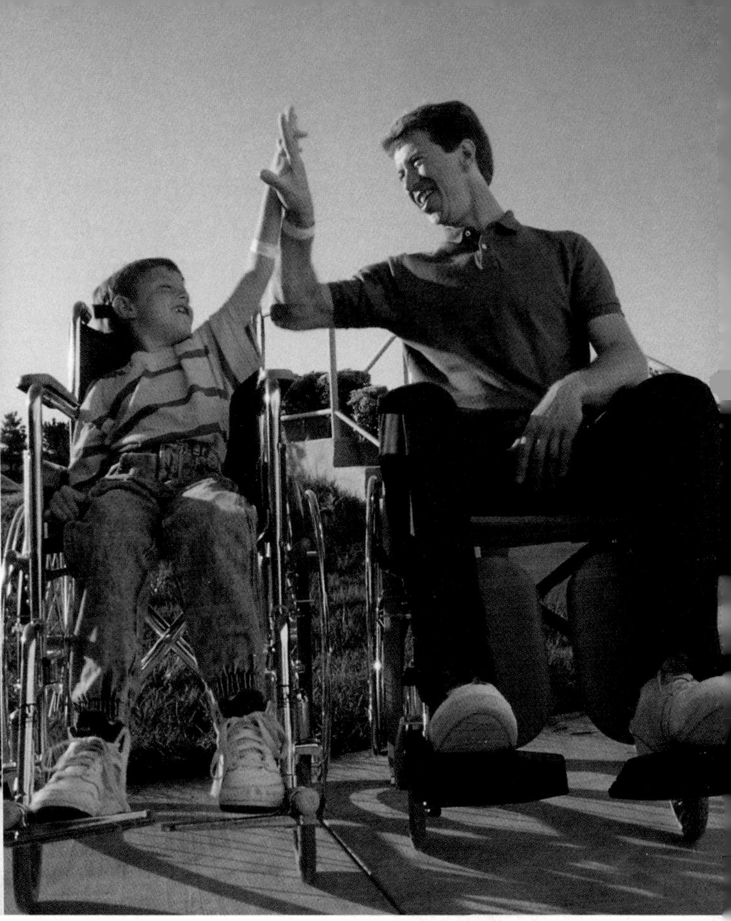

How can you exercise your brain? Use it! Use it at school and at play. Think some new thoughts and try some new games.

Your brain likes to be used. So, use your brain and keep it strong!

Glossary

brain the body organ inside the skull that works with the spinal cord and nerves to control, balance, and keep the body, mind, and emotions in order

brainstem the part of the brain that is in charge of automatic things, movement, digestion, and getting rid of waste

cerebellum the part of the brain that makes all the body parts work together to keep the body balanced

exercise body activity

forebrain the part of the brain that controls body temperature, emotions, information from the senses, memories, and thoughts

nervous system the system in the body made of the brain, spinal cord, and nerves that allows the body to think, remember, feel, and do things

skull bones inside the head that form together and protect the brain

spinal cord a column inside the back that connects the brain with the rest of the body

nerves little sensors throughout the body that send and receive messages